Faithonomics

Faithonomics

An Application of Biblical Truth to Times of Economic Crisis

K. Brad Stamm

RESOURCE *Publications* · Eugene, Oregon

FAITHONOMICS
An Application of Biblical Truth to Times of Economic Crisis

Resource Publications
An Imprint of Wipf and Stock Publishers
199 W. 8th Ave., Suite 3
Eugene, OR 97401

www.wipfandstock.com

ISBN 13: 978-1-61097-528-5

Manufactured in the U.S.A.

Contents

Preface

Without faith it is impossible to please God (Rom. 11:6). So it follows that no matter what we do, if it is not done in faith, it is not pleasing to him. No matter how seemingly meaningless our daily round of tasks, no matter the amount of drudgery that may be involved, we live for him. While Scripture makes clear again and again that our work does not save us, it can clearly bring honor to his name. And the same can be said of our intellectual lives. Is it a coincidence that the mandate to love God begins with the call to love him with our *minds*? Isn't that where our troubles always begin, in the mind? That's where temptation takes hold. That's where wanting something that isn't ours begins. That's where Jesus faced his temptations in the desert, dealing with power, physical hunger, and the most deadly of all, pride and its foundation of self-assurance. He tackled each situation successfully, quoting God's unique Word for that issue. The battle is in the mind; that's where it's staged. And that's why in the academy those who claim there is no battle are deceived. For without renewal in that part of our selves, every other aspect of us remains at some level in a fallen state. How do we know God's position on economic issues if we don't have his mind but instead depend on human wisdom? It is impossible without faith to please God, and faith comes by hearing and hearing by the Word of God. As Paul expressed it, "We have the mind of Christ" (1 Cor. 2:16).

Acknowledgments

I THINK mentors mean more as you move along in life, as have mine. Without the encouragement of Linwood Geiger of Eastern University, I would not be teaching. Without working side by side at Nyack College with the former CEO of JCPenney, Don Seibert, I would not understand how to get things done through people. Without being mentored by one of the nation's best professors and economists, Dominick Salvatore of Fordham University, I wouldn't understand what academic excellence is. Without watching my father, Kenneth E. Stamm, effectively manage and market a very successful bank in Ohio, I wouldn't understand the power of being charitable. And without my wife, Tami, my daughter, Sara, and my son, Ethan, I wouldn't understand that I am more than I could be but less than I should be. Without Jesus I am nothing but proud, but with him I am forever humbled because he gives me all things—and thus I owe him everything.

Introduction

I RECALL one summer day when my daughter, Sara, and I were on the back porch of the house I was renting at Nyack College outside of New York City. The house resembled a small chalet and had a beautiful view overlooking the Hudson River. I was reading *Essays on Economics and Economists* by R. H. Coase (1994), and she was reading *My First Bible*. She looked at me and asked, "Dad, what are you reading?" I replied, "I'm reading economics. What are you reading, Sara?" "I'm reading the Bible, Dad, and it has some economics in it."

This has become my view regarding the integration of economics with the Scriptures in the college classroom: look for ways to apply economics to the Scriptures in order to better understand both the passage and the economic principle involved, but don't try to make an economic interpretation of the Bible. Too many Christian economists and business professors make this mistake—and I do believe it is a mistake—because the primary intention of Scripture is to reveal Christ and his plan of redemption to us, not to convey economic principles. Once we see the Bible as an economic blueprint for living, we start down a path of economic legalism, along with a corresponding judgmental attitude.

Throughout this book I will give you examples that I use in my classroom and various speaking engagements. These examples have proven to be very popular with students, not because they are perfect but because they promote the exchange of ideas, both spiritual and academic. If the examples were perfect, this would assume a complete and clear understanding of both the Scriptures and economics, neither of which I can claim. At the end of each chapter you will find a section entitled "Food for Thought," which is intended to cause you to reflect on your own life and better understand your worldview. The other section is "Thought for Food," which lists resources, both spiritual and economic, for further reading. I am greatly indebted to Dr. Philip Bustrum, professor of religion at Cornerstone University, for his many and helpful suggestions of both Bible passages and Christian books to make this section much more valuable to the reader. I owe much to Tim Beals and Donna Huisjen at Credo Communications for making this book more cohesive, readable, and accurate. I also want to thank Christian Amondson and Robert Hand at Wipf & Stock Publishers for seeing this project through from beginning to end with such attention to detail along with an encouraging spirit.

For those looking for an analytical micro- or macro-economic study, this book will not suffice. And for those wanting a theology of economics, this book will also fall short. For the group that wants lessons in how to get rich, how to get out of debt, or other areas of personal finance, other sources will be more appropriate. My hope is that those wanting to learn something of economics via the Scriptures through a broadly evangelical view, and those wanting to learn something of God's character through an economic lens, will find the applications both interesting and useful. The book is not intended to be read in its entirety in a few sittings but one chapter at a time, allowing time to reflect on the issues at hand and in our hearts.

So welcome to an economist's view of various Scriptures passages. I pray that you will see him more clearly and walk with him more closely as you read my book.

1

The Candlestick Maker

THE JOB market for the last several years has been tight, with job losses throughout the country and weak employment continuing into the foreseeable future. Unemployment has approached levels nearly surpassing those set in the early 1980s. The broader nationwide unemployment index, known as U-6, which includes marginally-attached workers along with those employed part time for economic reasons, gives us a much more realistic picture of the "unemployed" and is several percentage points higher than the more popularly defined rate.

What is a college graduate or currently unemployed or underemployed person to do in this job market? You're out there as a somewhat homogenous commodity, in company with over 1.2 million others graduating with bachelor's degrees each spring, each attempting to obtain the same positions as fellow graduates. And this is not to mention the existing pool of millions who have lost their jobs or are changing career directions and looking for work. Career counselors advise applicants to differentiate themselves in some way so that prospective employers can tell them apart from other job seekers. I want to suggest, however, that while your vocation is important, it is not as important as our Christian calling to be engaged in God's work of reconciliation while on Earth (2 Cor. 5:16–21).

Let's take a look at three individuals in quite a different light from the way in which they were described in the over two-hundred-year-old English-language nursery rhyme.

THE BUTCHER

What if you've been trained at a particular university to be a butcher? If there is a movement away from eating beef for dietary or other reasons, the butcher may find herself out of work. What will that do to her self-esteem, and what will be her value in the eyes of society? The future for butchers appears to be quite bleak.

THE BAKER

Being a baker seems to be a good occupation. Almost everyone eats bread daily. However, bread is made from flour, flour is made from wheat, and the price of wheat has more than tripled in the past several years. Thus the baker goes out of business due to the high cost of production in addition to a certain percentage of people going on low-carbohydrate diets. So the baker's life now has less meaning because he too is unemployed.

THE CANDLESTICK MAKER

While the butcher and baker have lost their meaning in life due to a lack of demand for their products, the candlestick maker retains hers because we always need to find our way around in the dark. We always need a light to give us direction. We always need illumination to keep us from stumbling. So while we still have darkness on Earth, those who provide light will always be in demand. Possibly the butcher and baker should, at least as their avocation, go into the candle-making business to provide a living for themselves and help others.

It's important to understand that our primary calling is to the Lord; that we participate in his redemption work of bringing all persons to repentance and faith in his Son, Jesus Christ; that we worship no other gods; and that we love our family, friends, and even our enemies. Our other "callings" will invariably change, allowing us to serve him in new ways depending on choice and circumstances. So whether in prison or free, whether a banker or a barber, whether employed or unemployed, whether at a high or low income level, whether living near or far from our place of origin, we are always called to live according to Jesus's words in Luke 10:27: "Love the Lord your God with all your heart and with all your soul and with all your strength and with your entire mind," and "Love your neighbor as yourself." Thus the end goal of our academic pursuits is to love God more and to both spread and make an apology for his kingdom of truth and love, as did the apostle Paul—both near and far, in our vocations and in our avocations, among our friends and among those who dislike us.

FOOD FOR THOUGHT

- When you think about your "mission" in life, do you think primarily in terms of your job, your work within your church or voluntary organization, or your commitment to your family and friends?

- If you wrote out your life's "mission" five to ten years ago, how differently would it look if you wrote it today?

- If you were to lose your job, what would you have remaining?

THOUGHT FOR FOOD

- Godin, Seth. *Tribes*. New York: Portfolio, 2008.

- ———. *Linchpin*. New York: Portfolio, 2011.

- Guinness, Os. *The Call*. Nashville: Thomas Nelson, 2003. A biblical, practical, balanced, intriguing, and historical view of calling.

- Mankiw, N. Gregory. *Essentials of Economics*. Mason, OH: South-Western Cengage Learning, 2011.

- Wessels, Walter J. *Economics (Barron's Business Review)*. Hauppauge, NY: Barron's Educational Series, 2006.

2

The "Sin" of Wages

THE SCRIPTURES say that a worker deserves his wages. But is the CEO of the company equally deserving? The average pay for an executive in the United States is $11 million, more than three-hundred times what the typical worker makes. Contrast this with Japan, where the ratio of CEO to average worker pay is 16:1. Several heads of the financial firms that received more than $66 billion in the TARP (Troubled Asset Relief Program) government bailout package average $13 million in annual pay. And if you aren't an Ohio State University alum or fan and need one more reason not to like the Buckeyes, take note that their president is the highest paid in the nation at more than $1.5 million. (Perhaps it is because it is widely known that the president of Ohio State University is the highest paid in the country that he donated $220,000 to a scholarship fund.)

Economists make a strong case for paying people at an appropriate level. The theory, called "efficiency wages," has been studied by such notables as Nobel Prize winner Joseph Stiglitz. It has been shown that better-paid workers are healthier, more productive, less prone to turnover, and willing to put forth more effort. Organizations that pay higher wages also attract higher-quality workers. The focus created by today's business environment seems to be on executive compensation, with the burden for excessive pay falling on the workers and shareholders. This problem has not gone unnoticed. The Dodd-Frank Wall Street Reform and Consumer Protection Act, signed into law by President Obama in 2010, requires companies to disclose the pay gap within their organizations between CEO and employees. The objective is to lessen the gap by increasing transparency.

The reaction and response to disparity in wages comes not only from outside but also within the Christian community. Some Christian economists have suggested a society with no money, wages, or debt, in which all exchange is based on reciprocity (see *Calculated Futures* by Long, Fox, and York). Practical, everyday examples of these kinds of social exchanges include such activities as watching each other's children, providing meals for others, and shoveling snow for one another. So, for example, if you are a faculty member at Ohio State University, in exchange for grading another member's student essays, you might receive tickets to a Buckeyes games on the fifty-yard line.

No doubt there are gross inequities in pay between seniors and subordinates, but at the same time there is considerable societal, shareholder, and government pressure that provides a countervailing force to runaway executive compensation. The apostle Paul tells us that if we work for and to the Lord (1 Cor. 10:31), whether that work is "sacred" or "secular" in nature and whether we consider ourselves a lay person or in the "ministry," what we do—regardless of how we are treated or paid—is of great value. He is our rewarder as well as the judge of those who defraud laborers of their just wages (Mal. 3:5).

FOOD FOR THOUGHT

- Do you think that you are fairly paid? What is "fair pay"?

- In Jesus's story about the laborers in Matthew 20:1–16, each is paid the same wage, no matter what time they showed up to work. Is this parable a model for compensation, a lesson on what it truly means to be fair, or parenthetical to the issue of wages or economics?

THOUGHT FOR FOOD

- For a look at wage discrepancies between genders, see U.S. Department of Labor and U.S. Bureau of Labor Statistics, *Highlights of Women's Earnings in 2009*, June 2010, http://www.bls.gov/cps/cpswom2009.pdf.

- For income inequality among U.S. states, see Amanda Noss, "Household Income for States," September 2011, http://www.census.gov/prod/2011pubs/acsbr10-02.pdf.

- Long, D. Stephen, Nancy Ruth Fox, and Tripp York. *Calculated Futures: Theology, Ethics, and Economics.* Waco: Baylor University Press, 2007. See also my review of this book in *Faith and Economics* 54 (2009): 128–32.

3

Business: Minister of Good or Evil?

BUSINESS SEEMS to most of us to be quite incongruous with ministry, and there is considerable justification for holding this view. Many people identify businesspeople as greedy, arrogant capitalists whose main objective in life is to exploit those both near and far. When most people think of economics, what typically comes to mind is Adam Smith's "invisible hand," the premise that behavior motivated merely by individuals' self-interest can, and under the right conditions will, still lead to beneficial outcomes not merely for the individual(s) concerned but for others as well. This interpretation of Smith's work is generally overstated and misconstrued. In *The Wealth of Nations*, he says that "no society can surely be flourishing and happy of which the far greater part of the members are poor and miserable," a much more egalitarian stance than the self-centered money grabber outlook he is generally attributed to hold (see Smith, *Wealth of Nations* 1.1; see also Shiller and Shiller, "Economists as Worldly Philosophers"). While the more holistic view of Smith's works gives us some consolation as to what type of father he is to capitalism, there are far too numerous, recent, and close-to-home examples of people whose "love of money" does wreak havoc in their lives and the lives of others.

Bernie Madoff, the former chairman of NASDAQ, was sentenced to 150 years in prison for the largest Ponzi scheme in history, which bilked investors of $65 billion. And Kenneth Lay and Jeffrey Skilling, the "masterminds" behind the Enron fraud, as well as Bernie Ebbers of WorldCom, have all been convicted of securities fraud and conspiracy. Years earlier the junk-bond king Michael Milken was convicted after being indicted on ninety-eight counts of racketeering and securities fraud. There is an ongoing illusion that individuals won't be seen behind the corporate wall of protection and that they can thus proceed to push the limits of both pay and ethical boundaries—or keep stretching the ethical and pay rubber bands until they snap back or break. The parade of individual and corporate malfeasance is long and includes not only the above names but also such notables as Martha Stewart.

There is, happily, a new and countervailing force to this prevalence of business wrongdoing in which men and women seek to glorify the Lord through their business ventures. This movement of God has become so prominent that in 2004 the Lausanne Forum set as one of its objectives "to examine the obstacles, challenges, and opportunities to glorify God globally by furthering his kingdom through the strategy of business as mission." This spiritual movement is called by many names and comes in many forms, such as Business as Missions, Business as Ministry, and Business for Transformation.

Business can and should be a minister of good, not evil. Students who attend many Christian colleges are learning and believing that they can have a reason, not an excuse, for majoring in business because they can operate their businesses according to Christian principles. They can donate part of their profits to Christian organizations; follow godly hiring practices; refuse to discriminate against individuals, races, ethnicities, or genders; and travel to less-developed countries, helping indigenous groups set up sustainable businesses.

However, "business as ministry" goes well beyond providing economic relief and financing "Christian work." Its true purpose is the spiritual transformation, the salvation, of all stakeholders, including not only the employees but also all others within the economic and geographic reach of the enterprise. Many Christian college business programs sponsor seminars to help their students publicly identify with and affirm this new and exciting international movement of God within the business environment. The goal is to provide a firm foundation for students of what it means to do "business as ministry" and to invite to the campus guest lecturers who are currently engaged in marketplace ministry. Graduates may then effectively "go into the entire world and make disciples" through their vocational calling as business persons.

FOOD FOR THOUGHT

- Have society and the judicial system been too lenient or too harsh when it comes to Madoff, Ebbers, and others?

- Has your church adopted the concept of "business as ministry"? If not, do you think they would welcome or resist the idea? Why or why not?

- Should there be a distinct difference in the approach to business and economics at a Christian college or university? What explicit differences exist or would you anticipate?

THOUGHT FOR FOOD

- Business as Mission website: http://www .businessasmission.com/home.html.

- Chewning, Eby, John Wilmer Eby, and Shirley J. Roels. *Business through the Eyes of Faith*. New York: HarperCollins, 1990.

- Christian Business Faculty Association: http://cbfa .org/.

- Friedman, Benjamin M. "Economics: A Moral Inquiry with Religious Origins." *American Economic Review*, 101.3 (2011): 166–70.

- Johnson, C. Neal. *Business as Mission*. Downers Grove, IL: InterVarsity, 2009.

- Moreland, J. P., and Dallas Willard. *Love Your God with All Your Mind*. Colorado Springs: NavPress, 1997. The authors create a practical template for integrating not only faith and business but also faith and the other academic disciplines.

- Shiller, Robert, and Virginia Shiller. "Economists as Worldly Philosophers." *American Economic Review: Papers & Proceedings* 101.3 (2011): 171–75.

- Smith, Adam. *The Wealth of Nations*. 1776; New York: Oxford University Press, 2008.

- Stackhouse, Max L., Preston N. Williams, and Shirley J. Roels. *On Moral Business*. Grand Rapids: Eerdmans, 1995.

4

I've Made a "Mess of Me"—Please Bail Me Out!

IN THE last few years the word *bailout* has become commonplace. The investment banking firm Bear Stearns was bailed out by the U.S. Government for $29 billion and the insurance company AIG for $182 billion. Four hundred banks in the past few years have been bailed out by the FDIC at a cost of over $20 billion per year. In addition, partial government bailouts or buyouts include two fallen giants of industry and finance, GM and Citigroup. The not-so-lucky include the now bankrupt Lehman Brothers Holdings, saddled with $613 billion in debt.

Countries also get into financial difficulty, with Spain being cited as the first sovereign nation to go bankrupt in 1557. Mexico, South Korea, Indonesia, Thailand, Brazil, Russia, and more recently Ukraine and Hungary have been loaned large sums of money by the International Monetary Fund to stave off impending financial crises. Iceland essentially declared bankruptcy in October 2008, and Greece was bailed out for the first time in 2010 by the IMF and EU to the tune of $159 billion and then a second time in March 2011 for an additional $172 billion. Since 1800 there have been about two hundred instances of countries defaulting on their debt, as well as at least sixty-nine instances of major domestic defaults or restructurings since 1740. Walter Wriston, former CEO of Citibank, stated that "countries don't go bust." Well, they do . . . and they will.

Individuals are also enduring economic distress, as evidenced by over 1.5 million bankruptcy filings in 2010, a 9 percent increase over 2009 and a 35 percent increase over 2008. Equally dramatic were the 1.05 million homes foreclosed on in 2010. A record 2.9 million homes received foreclosure notices in the same year, setting another record. Given the approximate $2.5 trillion in consumer credit extended to you and me and a total of $11.5 trillion in household debt, we should not be surprised to see an escalation in the number of personal bankruptcies and foreclosures. College education adds to these costs. On average, students graduate with $25,000 of debt—not that astounding given that the annual cost of public education is $15,000 and of private education $32,000. Total nationwide student debt totals $1 trillion.

While debt becomes an increasing burden for college students, there are times when what they need is not an economic but an academic bailout. They may have done poorly in a course, resulting in a grade point average (GPA) in need of restructuring. One remedy for students is to take the course over again. Another approach is for them to transfer to another college (their course credits transferring while their grades do not). These "bailouts" aren't complete or entirely sufficient because the old grade still remains on their transcript, and, typically, only courses in which they receive a C- or higher are transferable. But this approach does provide something of a fresh start.

A bailout that is sufficient and complete and does provide a brand new start in life is one in which I turn over all of my mistakes and my deficiencies, whether inherited, premeditated, or involuntary, to Christ. I can truly begin again, just as though I were being born a second time, exonerated from all of my past sins and free to serve and love. The second greatest benefit of this spiritual bailout is that I now have the privilege of telling others about this eternal rescue so that they too can share this new life that none of us deserve.

FOOD FOR THOUGHT

- How do you feel about economically troubled countries being bailed out by the International Monetary Fund, European Union , and so on? In your opinion, does this give the country breathing room to start over, or does it give them a license to continue in their bad economic behavior?

- When someone forgives you, how do you respond? Are you more likely to forgive others, or are others more likely to forgive you? What are some of the consequences of unforgiveness?

- Are bankruptcy laws unfair? That is, do they promote irresponsible behavior? Does forgiveness of sin promote bad behavior?

THOUGHT FOR FOOD

- For more information on consumer debt, see http://www.federalreserve.gov.

- For "Debt to the Penny," see http://www .treasurydirect.gov/NP/BPDLogin?application=np.

- For U.S. deficit data, see http://fms.treas.gov/mts/ overview.html.

- For more information on the International Monetary Fund and its lending procedures, see http://www.imf.org/external/index.htm.

- For information on foreign holders of U.S. debt, see http://www.treasury.gov/resource-center/data-chart-center/tic/Documents/mfh.txt.

- For an insightful history of debt crises, see Carmen Reinhart and Kenneth Rogoff, *This Time Is Different* (Princeton: Princeton University Press, 2011).

- If you want a book on forgiveness, see Philip Yancey, *What's So Amazing about Grace?* (Grand Rapids: Zondervan, 2002).

5

A Christmas Story

MARKETING DEPARTMENTS and public relations firms are quite good at getting us to anticipate a new version of the iPhone, a sequel to a movie such as Star Wars, Harry Potter, or Lord of the Rings, or a new car model. Typical shopping experiences can turn into frenzies during the holiday season when prices are advertised as being significantly reduced or at cost. Agents, managers, record companies, and concert promoters are always hard at work to build momentum for an artist's upcoming tour in hopes of sellout crowds. The objective is to keep us always on the edge of our seats so that initial sales for those early adopters are significant enough to build momentum to provide mass appeal.

Our expectations often affect our attitudes and actions. For example, if you think the price of gasoline is going to increase within the next few days, you will probably fill up your tank today in order to save money. Or if parents are able to lock in college tuition for their child several years in advance, they might do so if they expect tuition to increase by the time their son or daughter is ready to enter the institution.

Another example is that of a farmer expecting the price of corn to go up next year and therefore putting more of his acreage into corn production to benefit from the anticipated higher prices. Interestingly, expectations can beget more expectations. Rising prices can potentially turn into even higher prices because people build these escalating costs into their future expectations. When workers are faced with higher prices for the goods they buy, they increase their wage demands to meet these rising costs. Home prices are an example of this because they tend to increase annually, causing buyers to embed these increases into their thinking, even though this is not always justified. And, of course, the opposite could happen: as prices decline the expectation can be that they will decline further, a pattern of thinking that does in fact induce further reductions, as evidenced beginning in 2006. Generally, prices are balanced out by supply and demand and tend toward equilibrium; however, the opposite can occur when prices continue to somewhat irrationally go down or up, such as we see in stock market bubbles or crashes.

Nor is the topic of expectations unique to economics. In the behavioral sciences there is a theory called the Pygmalion effect, which is essentially a self-fulfilling prophecy. Employees and students will perform according to the expectations of their supervisors or teachers. Low expectations breed low performance, while high expectations on the part of those who are leading and teaching result in higher performance.

Expectations also have religious significance. The Advent season is a reminder both of our commemoration of the first coming of the Messiah and of our anticipation of the second coming of Christ. These are not self-fulfilling, Pygmalion-type expectations but rather prophecies from Scripture already fulfilled and to be fulfilled. The birth of Christ was not of human will but initiated by his Father. Moreover, while the second coming is greatly anticipated by many, the exact timing is solely the prerogative of the Father.

The Christmas story, perhaps history's greatest expectation of a "new release," was written long ago, fulfilled by divine appointment, and is all about the benefits that accrue to us. It requires no investment on our part other than our response to the call to repent and turn to God so that our sins may be totally wiped out (Acts 3:19). This story is one of peace, joy, and right standing with God, certainly something to be merry about.

FOOD FOR THOUGHT

- Have you ever been caught up in a speculative "bubble"? How do we keep ourselves from following the crowd, whether the issue at hand is stocks, housing, or the latest trends?

- What are the benefits of expecting Christ's return to earth? Can this expectation also turn into a speculative bubble?

THOUGHT FOR FOOD

- For more on rational expectations, see the work of Thomas Sargent and Christopher Sims, winners of the 2011 Nobel Prize in Economics, http://www.nobelprize.org/nobel_prizes/economics/laureates/2011/.

- For a look at behavioral economics, see George A. Akerlof and Robert Shiller, *Animal Spirits* (Princeton: Princeton University Press, 2009); and Robert Shiller, *Irrational Exuberance* (New York: Crown, 2005).

6

Homo Reciprocans?

ONE OF my students asked me under what circumstances I am happiest, and I responded that it is usually when I am affirmed by others or affiliated with people who instill in me the sense that I have value. The times that most of us feel at our worst are when we're neglected or lack support from a person or group.

When we say hello to someone coming from the opposite direction on the sidewalk, most of us would expect them to reciprocate, but the reality is that they often look down at the pavement, saying nothing. You could as easily be in a small midwestern town as in New York City for this to happen. I've lived in both. Maybe this is a result of shyness. Or possibly these individuals are preoccupied with what is going on in their heads. I want to suggest, however, that we do not inherently function as *homo reciprocans*—that is, we are not predisposed to taking interest in others and being cooperative, as that model would suggest. The *homo reciprocans* view of humanity is quite unlike the model of *homo economicus*, of which Adam Smith's self-interested, rational human being whose end is himself is representative.

Being noticed by others can be a motivator; it can elicit effort. Abraham Maslow's dated but still relevant hierarchy of needs pyramid puts self-esteem and respect by others second from the top (see Maslow, "Theory of Human Motivation"). These conditions, according to Maslow, are necessary for human motivation. Several years ago my family and I boarded a plane in New York for Los Angeles, and a well-known folk artist on his way to first class stopped by our row to say hello to my then five-year-old daughter Sara. This made both her day and her parents'. A few years later I was at a major conference at which a Nobel Prize winner needed someone to simply place his transparencies on top of the projector's surface. My PhD mentor, the organizer of the session, spotted and called me out of an audience filled with economists from all over the world, along with national media representatives, to take on the task. Recognition can inspire.

Drew Carey, a fellow native of Ohio, hosts *The Price Is Right*. The game show works not simply due to the giveaways, such as expensive cars and exotic vacations, but because people from the audience are somewhat randomly called to "come on down" to the stage; from a sea of several hundred expectant contestants, a few will end up with a chance to bid on the final showcase. Recognition brings importance, value, and affirmation.

Jesus himself received affirmation and recognition from his Father. Matthew tells us that a voice sounded from heaven, saying, "You are my Son, whom I love; with you I am well pleased." Likewise, the Son gives attention to, serves, recognizes, and affiliates with us. He calls each of us by name out of the sea of humanity, just as he called Zacchaeus from the sycamore tree, bidding us to not only follow him but to become members of his family. Jesus both identifies us and identifies with us.

The next time you're walking down the sidewalk, consider greeting the person coming toward you. Jesus mercifully greets each of us, day in and day out, always waiting for us to look up, away from our self-absorption, and respond to his call.

FOOD FOR THOUGHT

- How does it feel when you go unnoticed? Can you think of a situation in which someone of importance recognized and acknowledged you?

- How do you balance your need to be recognized with the ongoing challenge to avoid conceit?

- Is saying "hello" when passing others merely politeness, or can it be more than that?

THOUGHT FOR FOOD

- For Maslow's hierarchy of needs, see A. H. Maslow, "A Theory of Human Motivation," *Psychological Review* 50 (1943): 370–96.

- For a readable perspective on our importance to God, see the classic by Francis Schaeffer, *No Little People* (Wheaton: Crossway, 2003).

- Scripture references: Genesis 1:26–27; Psalm 139:14; Job 33:4.

7

Is It Worth It?

Economists are well known for looking at things in terms of their costs and benefits. But without a proper worldview, this approach can have quite disturbing results. For example, some have suggested that the legalization of abortion has led to a decrease in the crime rate. The ungodly policy implication of this suggestion is that the cost to society of allowing these potential criminals to be born is greater than the socio-economic benefits that will result from their time here on earth. Thus, according to the "amoral" economist or businessperson, these individuals should be aborted, given the odds that they will lead unproductive lives.

Another cost-benefit example, clearly not as significant as the life-and-death situation above, is whether getting a college degree is truly worth the money. People have many different perspectives on the costs and benefits of higher education given the annual costs that often become a financial burden to both the students and their parents. Some families and prospective students posit that Christian higher education in particular isn't worth the cost. After all, in your four years at a Christian college or university, tuition plus room and board might cost well over $100,000, and you will walk away at graduation with a diploma in one hand and significant debt obligations in the other. When you add to that the dismal employment picture in many areas of the country, the challenge of paying back your loans reaches far into the future.

Is a Christian college education worth the cost? In my opinion, yes! Both from my perspective and from my experience, it is well worth the investment, with the benefits far outweighing the costs. With a bachelor's degree you will earn on average $1 million more over the course of your working life than someone who has not gone to college. Even if you are a waiter or waitress, your wages on average will be 34 percent higher with a bachelor's degree than without. Your opportunity for both initial employment and subsequent advancement increases significantly. Your network of friends and other social relationships expands. Your relationships with faculty, staff, and administrators open the door for lifelong mentoring opportunities. Most important, your spiritual life, which has been nurtured at a Christian institution of higher education, your mind, which has been set on Christ, your integrity and sincerity of heart, which have been encouraged by those around you, and your eternal perspectives, which will prevent you from making short-run, costly mistakes, will save you a great deal of future heartache and perhaps even money. Thus your personal value and worth to the kingdom of God will increase, extending through eternity.

The cost of not attending college is great, and I firmly believe that when all the spiritual dimensions are included, the cost of not attending a Christian university is even greater.

FOOD FOR THOUGHT

- What's wrong with making decisions merely on a cost/benefit analysis basis? What other factors should be included in our decision making?

- Why don't more families and students consider attending a Christian college or university? What could be done to remove some of those obstacles?

- What differences are there between Christian and "secular" institutions of higher learning? What differences would you expect would exist between the two?

THOUGHT FOR FOOD

- Carnevale, Anthony P., and Stephen J. Rose. "The Undereducated American." Georgetown University Center on Education and the Workforce. June 26, 2011, http://www9.georgetown.edu/grad/gppi/hpi/cew/pdfs/undereducatedamerican.pdf.

- Greenstone, Michael, and Adam Looney, "College Is Expensive but Still a Smart Choice," Brookings Institution. August 15, 2011, http://www.brookings.edu/opinions/2011/0815_college_greenstone_looney.aspx. An economic report concerning the financial benefits of a college education.

- Levitt, Steven, and Stephen Dubner. *Freakonomics.* New York: HarperCollins, 2009. This book provides both interesting and somewhat controversial applications of economics to real world situations.

- Ringenberg, William C. *The Christian College: A History of Protestant Higher Education in America.* Grand Rapids: Baker Academic, 2006. A wonderful background of and rationale for Christian higher education.

- See the U.S. Department of Education "College Affordability and Transparency Center" to compare the actual cost of attending public and private colleges across the country: http:// collegecost.ed.gov/catc/Default.aspx

- For a list of Christian colleges, see http://www .cccu.org.

- Scripture references: Luke 16:15; John 15:4–9; Philippians 4:1; James 2:17.

8

Money or the Messiah: Please Choose One

THERE IS nothing more important to most people than economics. Individuals make decisions on whether to get married or stay single based on tax deductions, living expenses, and health plans. The desire for gay couples to marry is similarly influenced by economics; they are interested in the same pecuniary benefits as those enjoyed by heterosexual couples.

Your profession greatly determines who you are in the eyes of the world. What people think of you is dictated by the amount of money you earn, which firm you are with, what college you graduated from, what part of town you live in, and who your friends are. If you attend a party and are introduced to a stranger, one of the first things they might ask is, "What is your line of work?" In essence they are asking, "How much money do you make, what type of car do you drive, how big is your house, and where is your vacation home?"

From the time you are conceived until your financial estate is settled, it is all about money. Your prenatal development is closely monitored to determine whether you are a viable economic unit. If the projected cost to maintain you throughout life is greater than the benefits that will be derived from your existence, your father and mother, with the advice of well-seasoned medical counselors, can decide whether you are worth bringing to term.

As you grow older, you continue making decisions from an economic perspective. The cost of growing old, including prescription drugs and long-term care, is escalating, and the ability to cover those expenses, particularly if you are on a fixed income, is diminishing. A typical funeral runs about $7,000. Alternatively, you can choose a less expensive form of burial, such as cremation, at about one-fourth the cost. In some areas of the country, if you are indigent, you even have the option of being buried in a "potters field." If the prevailing worldview does not place significant value on the elderly, and the estimated cost of extending your life is greater than the benefits to be derived by society from your continued existence, you may eventually find yourself to be a candidate for euthanasia. While to some this might seem like science fiction, the final version of the 2011 health care legislation, only to be amended at the last minute, stated that Medicare will cover "voluntary advance care planning" to discuss end-of-life treatment and advice on how to prepare an "advance directive" if the patient becomes too ill to make their own health decisions.

Without Jesus, economics would be our god. Without the underlying belief and understanding that Jesus is the source of all truth—that he *is* in fact the truth—and that nothing makes sense outside of him, economics will prevail; it will dominate our thinking, our living, and our practices. Our values will be determined, at best, on the basis of whether something is "good" for us or for those in our circle of concern, or on whether we are causing some type of harm or inconvenience to others. In addition, since those without Christ have no clear concept of eternity, their decisions are made on a temporal basis, excluding God's eternal perspectives on righteousness and judgment.

Having a Christocentric worldview, I believe, means putting money in its rightful place as a means of serving others, not as a measure of success. But even a "biblical" view may not be the correct interpretation unless its understanding is guided by the Spirit of God. It is becoming increasingly evident that many in the United States and elsewhere have put their money in a wrongful place, in a god who requires continuous sacrifices that end up making us look less like Jesus and more like sinful humanity.

FOOD FOR THOUGHT

- Do you think it is true that we are judged by our economic status? Is this less true for some age groups than for others? What do the Scriptures say regarding our view of others, whether from an economic or a cultural standpoint?

- What are some safeguards to keep us from letting economics dominate our decision making?

- What type of process should we go through with beginning- and end-of-life decisions?

THOUGHT FOR FOOD

- Bing, Charles C. *Lordship Salvation.* Maitland, FL: Xulon, 2010.

- Grudem, Wayne. *Making Sense of Salvation.* Grand Rapids: Zondervan, 2011.

- Kapic, Kelly M. *God So Loved, He Gave: Entering the Movement of Divine Generosity.* Grand Rapids: Zondervan, 2010.

- MacArthur, John. *The Gospel according to Jesus: What Is Authentic Faith?* Grand Rapids: Zondervan, 2008.

- Scripture references: Matthew 6:33; 11:28–30; 19:23–24; Luke 12:15, 34; Acts 20:18–21; Hebrews 6:1; James 2:17; 1 Timothy 3:2–3; 6:3–5, 9, 17.

9

The Economics of Abortion and Bill Bennett's Gambling Problem

A FEW years ago on September 28, I was in the audience at the meeting of the Economics Club in a major midwestern city. The crowd became unusually silent when Stephen Levitt began discussing his research findings—that the legalization of abortion in the United States has led to a decrease in the crime rate. No one in the room directed a question to the speaker on this topic. No one voiced an opinion suggesting that his research methods might have been suspect. No one questioned the theory itself that abortion and crime are linked closely together, and particularly linked to abortions by mothers whose children are most likely to be at risk for future crime. This group, according to this author of *Freakonomics*, includes teenagers, unmarried women, and black women. All were silent at that meeting on September 28.

I too was silent. It was one of those times when the conscience was awakened, the heart pounded, and the conviction to do the right thing mounted, but the willingness to speak out, to take a position, and to contradict another's opinion got swallowed up by personal pride, peer pressure, and potential embarrassment. Stephen Levitt, a professor at the University of Chicago and an MIT graduate, is coauthor of the bestseller *Freakonomics*, a highly successful book that popularizes economics and in fact has been given credit for increasing the number of students interested in majoring in economics in college. Levitt's sometimes questionable research methods result in such absurd but interesting and applicable topics as "What do school teachers and sumo wrestlers have in common?" "How is the Ku Klux Klan like a group of real-estate agents?" and "Why do drug dealers still live with their moms?" The book owes at least some of its success, I believe, to the chapter on the relationship between the crime rate and Roe v. Wade, the 1973 Supreme Court decision, which in most cases outlawed states from violating a woman's right to choose to terminate a pregnancy. This research was first presented in Levitt's paper (coauthored with John Donohue) titled "The Impact of Legalized Abortion on Crime," published in 2001 by the *Quarterly Journal of Economics*.

Levitt's methods and theories have attracted critiques and comments both from within and outside the economics discipline, the last and most prominent criticism coming from William Bennett, host of the radio talk show *Morning in America*. Bennett was President Reagan's Secretary of Education and drug czar under former President Bush, and is author of *The Book of Virtues*.

I have been disheartened by Levitt's theory and research methods for several years ever since he released his findings suggesting that the Roe v. Wade decision led to a decline in the crime rate. For many semesters I have guided my economics classes through various discussions on the economics of abortion as it relates to Levitt's work. Each semester my students dialogue and debate Levitt and Donohue's rationale, question the $30 billion in economic benefits that the authors claim the country has received due to Roe v. Wade, ponder the likely eugenic policy implications of such irrational thought, and at times become inflamed by the discriminatory nature of the work done by the professors from the University of Chicago and Stanford.

Levitt and Donohue contend that as much as fifty percent of the reduction in crime in the 1990s can be attributed to the sharp increase in abortions after Roe v. Wade. Fewer crimes are committed today, they say, because the babies who would have grown up to be criminals have not been allowed to live. And this reduction in crime "appears to be attributable to higher rates of abortion by mothers whose children are most likely to be at risk for future crime." This group, according to the researchers and as I have already indicated, includes teenagers, unmarried women, and black women.

Most economists presume that their research and methodology are amoral. This is ludicrous. Facts and research are full of values and morals. We choose what to study. We create the hypotheses. We develop the theories. We look for the evidence to support the preconceived theories. We decide the type of research methodology. And then we determine how to deliver the results. Stephen Levitt chose the topic, created the theory, found the facts to support the theory, used the econometric methods to academically justify the theory, and selected the delivery method to communicate his findings. His work is biased, theoretically unsound, full of incorrect presuppositions, void of morals, and yet very interesting to a public that apparently is easily tantalized by economic stories of drug dealers and their mothers, the relationship between the Ku Klux Klan and realtors, and the economics of abortion.

Enter William Bennett with his criticism of Levitt during his Salem Broadcasting radio show, on which he responded facetiously and sarcastically to a listener's question that referred to Levitt's theory relating crime to abortion. Now Mr. Bennett is known for taking gambles, and in this case he lost big with the public, the Democrats, and even the White House by saying that if we really wanted to reduce crime, we "could abort every black baby in this country."

Now remember, this is exactly what Levitt has concluded. This is Levitt's theory, not Bill Bennett's, but Bennett takes the heat for his flippant remarks. It is Levitt's research, not Bennett's, but Bennett receives the media's contempt. William Bennett's response to the listener was in fact a futile, thoughtless, insensitive, untimely, and self-destructive attempt to counter Levitt's abortion argument.

All life is valuable. All life is redeemable—even the criminal's. All babies have the right to live and later choose whether they want to grow up to be a rap star, a Tea Party member, a Wal-Mart greeter, or a professor of economics. None of us are perfect; therefore, according to Stephen Levitt, it's just as possible that all deserve to be aborted. That is in fact the logical conclusion of eugenics. It certainly would decrease the crime rate in the United States if none of us were allowed to get past the first trimester. But this "would be impossible, ridiculous, and morally reprehensible," the exact words William Bennett used to describe his own ungodly remark in the very same breath he made it.

Os Guinness reminds us that if we were to truly comprehend that only one Person's approval in the audience matters, then our attitude in regard to all others in the crowd should be, "I have nothing to prove, nothing to gain, and nothing to lose." Silent no more.

FOOD FOR THOUGHT

- Why do we fear what others might think or say? And what are some steps to take that will help us be true to our convictions not only inwardly but outwardly, in speech and action?

- Should public figures such as Bill Bennett be held to different standards? Why are some people extended more grace and others less when it comes to blunders such as Bennett's, or other indiscretions?

- Do we often read books, view internet sites, watch movies, and listen to speeches without discerning what lies behind the statements, ideas, and theories?

THOUGHT FOR FOOD

- Levitt, Steven, and Stephen Dubner. *Freakonomics*. New York: HarperCollins, 2009.

- Mitchell, C. Ben, Edmund D. Pellegrino, Jean Bethke Elshtain, John F. Kilner, and Scott Rae. *Biotechnology and the Human Good*. Washington, DC: Georgetown University Press, 2007.

- Moreland, J. P., and William Craig. *Philosophical Foundations for a Christian Worldvi*ew. Downers Grove, IL: InterVarsity, 2003.

- Novak, David. *The Sanctity of Human Life*. Washington, DC: Georgetown University Press, 2009.

- Soulen, R. Kendall, and Linda Woodhead. *God and Human Dignity*. Grand Rapids: Eerdmans, 2006.

- Tada, Joni Eareckson, and Nigel M. de S. Cameron. *How to Be a Christian in a Brave New World*. Grand Rapids: Zondervan, 2006.

- Scripture references: Genesis 2:7; Deuteronomy 30:16; Acts 17:23–25; 1 Timothy 6:13–14.

10

Schizophrenia

A s an economist, the notion exists in the back of my mind (far, far in the back) that I could win the Nobel Prize. My students could easily attest that this is no small delusion on my part, and I heartily agree. But the dream is still there, awaiting the grandiose theory and associated hard work necessary to accomplish such a feat.

I've had the opportunity to hear in person many Nobel winners, including James Heckman, Lawrence Klein, Robert Lucas, Douglass North, Paul Krugman, and Joseph Stiglitz, the 2001 recipient. You probably haven't heard of any of these distinguished men. The best-known Nobel winner would more than likely be the brilliant but schizophrenic game-theory mathematician John Nash, made famous in the Oscar-winning movie *A Beautiful Mind*, starring Russell Crowe and Jennifer Connelly. I have never met Nash, but my professor's wife at Fordham University wrote the book that was the basis for the movie (only two degrees of separation, for those of you who are counting).

THE MAIN EVENT

A few years ago in January I attended the prestigious American Economic Association meeting in Washington, DC, where my PhD mentor, Dominick Salvatore, chaired one of the most popular sessions. Martin Feldstein, Harvard professor and former National Bureau of Economic Research chair, along with Lawrence Summers, former secretary of the Treasury and former president of Harvard University, and Joseph Stiglitz, the 2001 Nobel Prize winner, were the speakers.

When Stiglitz approached the podium to speak, no one showed up to take care of his overhead slides (Nobel laureates are not known for their technological prowess). Dr. Salvatore quickly took charge, standing up, facing the standing-room-only crowd and peered throughout the audience until he found a former student: me.

I walked nervously to the front of the room to lend a hand and proceeded to turn the overhead slides at the cuing of Professor Stiglitz. The task absolutely delighted me. It brought me great joy not only to be serving the renowned Joseph Stiglitz but also to be pleasing my mentor, Dominick Salvatore. It brought me joy because I am well aware of Stiglitz's significant contributions to the economics profession and because I could now give something back, albeit very small. Nonetheless, my minimal contribution still amounted to giving something back to an individual who had given me so much, both in and outside the classroom.

WASHING FEET

Jesus commands us to love one another and assures us that by doing so we will have complete joy (John 15:9–17). When we honestly acknowledge the significance of others, we will gladly serve them (Phil. 2:3). And when we submit ourselves to the lordship of the Father of those servants, we will want to please him, our Supreme Mentor. Thus we can attest that joy comes from serving, which lovingly evolves from an acknowledgement of the worth of those around us in obedience to the One who created us.

FOOD FOR THOUGHT

- Why is "washing feet" so difficult for many of us?
- What are the consequences of esteeming others better than ourselves?
- What is the importance of having a mentor (or mentors) in your life?

THOUGHT FOR FOOD

- Butt, Howard E. *The Velvet Covered Brick.* New York: Harper & Row, 1973.
- Nasar, Sylvia. *A Beautiful Mind.* New York: Simon & Schuster, 1998.
- Scripture references: Matthew 20:25–28; Mark 9:35–37; Romans 15:1–3; Philippians 2:3–8.

11

Mary or Martha Stewart? A Reflection of Society

THE PARADE of corporate malfeasance continues to grow and includes such notables as AIG, Arthur Andersen, Enron, and WorldCom along with the numerous brokerage firms that gave incorrect information to their clients to increase share prices and churn their clients' accounts. Perhaps the grand marshal of the parade is Martha Stewart, known in the past as the matriarch of all homemakers but now also known for her indictment in 2004 alleging involvement in selling shares of Imclone with inside information, which violated U.S. Securities and Exchange Commission rules.

It is a prosecutorial strategy to expose high profile individuals such as Ms. Stewart and, of earlier years, Leona Helmsley, in order to discourage the rest of us from even considering such heinous crimes. Criminalizing the celebrity is similar to ticketing those who drive over the speed limit, endangering the lives of others and themselves. If they are stopped by the police, the flashing lights and subsequent fine are intended to dissuade the rest of us from doing the same. The problem is that once we have slowed down to both appraise the speeder's humiliating situation and protect ourselves from a similar entrapment, we continue down the highway at the same excessive speed we were traveling before witnessing the person caught in their sin. We don't identify with the fine allotted to the violator, nor do we, for any length of time, remember the consequences of their actions. More regulation (in this case, police surveillance) would certainly help, but society can't function well in the long run unless there is a conscious effort on the part of individuals to do the right things in the public, private, and political arenas of life.

Christians are often no different in their business dealings from those we see paraded on the talk shows of CNN and Fox. We succumb to the financial temptations of short-term gain just as the Martha Stewarts do, but generally we are less conspicuous to the public eye. We can therefore seemingly hide our actions and suppress our consciences, bringing us a false sense of peace that masks the underlying unethical behavior.

Martha Stewart was too busy worrying about turning old coffee grounds into Christmas ornaments and should have been more like Mary, quietly listening to the Master, contemplating her life and thinking about reality from an eternal perspective. If I see myself as an eternal being who will at some point face the judgment of God, my actions will be radically modified in the temporal arena. I can't hold out, waiting for society to pass judgment, even with its wavering moral perspective. Instead I must daily judge myself in light of the Scriptures and ask those around me whom I respect to be honest with me if they sense impropriety in the way I conduct my business or personal life.

FOOD FOR THOUGHT

- What can be done about corporate malfeasance?
- Are celebrities unduly targeted and victims of entrapment?
- When the media focuses on, if not becomes obsessive in, its coverage of large scandals, celebrity or not, does it deter us from doing the same?

THOUGHT FOR FOOD

- Fairlie, Henry. *The Seven Deadly Sins Today.* Notre Dame: University of Notre Dame Press, 1979.
- Leviticus 25:43; Deuteronomy 24:14; Proverbs 22:16; Jeremiah 22:13–17; Malachi 3:5; Luke 12:22–31.

12

Left Behind

THERE IS a considerable amount of controversy surrounding the quasi-fictional Left Behind series by Tim LaHaye and Jerry Jenkins, and even more debate about whether the eschatological view of the "rapture" of the saints—while leaving the unrighteous "behind"—is accurate. Since I'm an economist and not a Bible scholar, I'll leave that discussion to the initiated. What I do know is that Christ will return to this earth and that I am to live a self-controlled, upright, and godly life until that happens (Titus 2:12–13).

THE ECONOMIC RAPTURE

In the United States there have been periods of significant and rapid economic expansion such as the 1980s and 1990s. There also have been eleven downturns in the economy since the 1940s, each having its own uniqueness in depth, longevity, and length of recovery.

From an economic standpoint, many people in the U.S. economy had been "raptured" from unemployment, poverty, and low standards of living over the years. However, we are quick to forget, unwilling to recognize, or naïve to the fact that while stock prices might be higher and unemployment rates are relatively low for those who have college degrees, not everyone today is experiencing economic prosperity, nor will they participate equally in economic recoveries.

WHO ARE THOSE LEFT BEHIND?

The United States in 2011 was home to more than 14 million unemployed people. To be classified as unemployed, one must be eighteen years old or older and have been looking for work. This figure doesn't include those who have been discouraged and stopped seeking employment, nor does it include those who have taken part-time jobs or are only marginally employed. If we broaden the scope to include these groups—the result of which would be known as the U-6 unemployment rate—the number would be significantly higher at 24.85 million people (16.2 percent).

The number of Americans living in poverty is the greatest in over fifty years and is now close to 14.3 percent, or 44 million people, while the median household income is in decline. The worsening economic conditions fell heaviest on midwesterners and nonwhites according to the Census Bureau. In addition, the gap between rich and poor is now the widest on record. The share of wealth held by the richest fifth of American households increased by 2.2 percentage points to 87.2 percent. The wealthiest 1 percent of U.S. households had a net worth that was 225 times greater than the median or typical household's net worth in 2009. This is the highest ratio on record. Incomes for the top 1 percent of households have grown 275 percent while only 18 percent for the bottom fifth of households. The Pew Research Center also reported that the median wealth of white households is twenty times that of black households and eighteen times that of Hispanic households.

A PIECE OF BREAD WILL BUY A BAG OF GOLD

Food insecurity, defined as not always having access to enough food to meet basic needs, is reported by the U.S. Department of Agriculture (USDA). In 2010, 14.5 percent of U.S. households (17.2 million) were food insecure, meaning that at some time during the year they had difficulty providing enough food for all members due to insufficient resources. The percentage was essentially unchanged from 2009 (14.7 percent), remaining at the highest level observed since food security surveys were initiated in 1995. Many households have sought additional resources from public and private sources. Since 2001 the number of households that reported obtaining emergency food from a food pantry has continued to rise each year over the previous twelve months. The largest increase occurred between 2007 and 2009, when households using food pantries rose by 44 percent, from 3.9 to 5.6 million households.

The USDA reported that food insecurity among children was more than twice as prevalent among households headed by black and Hispanic persons as among those

headed by white non-Hispanics. (See http://www.ers.usda.
gov/publications/eib56/eib56.pdf.)

I WAS HUNGRY AND YOU GAVE ME
SOMETHING TO EAT

Jesus said that one sign of the end of the age would be that
the love of many people would grow cold (Matt. 24:12). It
seems all too common for working people to blame economic misfortune on a person's unwillingness to pick themselves up by their own bootstraps. This is sometimes the
case; however, I think this attitude is reflective of the "cold
hearts" to which Jesus referred and of which he warned. I
suggest that we continue giving generously to the hungry,
needy, and economically disadvantaged in the United States
and throughout the world, not second-guessing the origin
of their need but responding to it in a godly, upright fashion
through organizations such as Compassion International,
World Relief, and a myriad of others that administer health,
hope, and education to a growing number of people who
have been left behind in a dark cloud of economic despair
and hunger.

FOOD FOR THOUGHT

- What obligation does society have to those without
  sufficient food and other necessities? What is it not
  obligated to do?

- Should we primarily be concerned about those
  in need in our own country, or should we focus
  first on the rest of the world considering that

malnutrition and starvation is worse elsewhere?

- Should economic equality be a goal of society?
What is your interpretation of Acts 2:42–47
regarding the fellowship of those early believers?

- Is the phrase "God helps those who help
themselves" biblical?

THOUGHT FOR FOOD

- For government data on unemployment, see http://
bls.gov.

- For government data on the general economy, see
http://bea.gov.

- For Census data on income, poverty, and other
statistics, see: http://www.census.gov.

- For data on food insecurity see the U.S.
Department of Agriculture, http://www.ers.usda
.gov/Briefing/FoodSecurity.

- Allegretto, Sylvia A. *The State of Working America's
Wealth*. 2011. A somewhat partisan but factual
view on disparity.

- Cox, W. Michael, and Richard Alm. *Myths of
Rich and Poor*. New York: Basic Books, 1999. A
somewhat dated but countervailing point of view.

- Nord, Mark, Alisha Coleman-Jensen, Margaret
Andrews, and Steven Carlson. *Household Food
Security in the United States, 2009*. ERR-108 (2010).

- Sider, Ronald J. *Rich Christians in an Age of*

Hunger: Moving from Affluence to Generosity.
Nashville: Thomas Nelson, 2005.

- Scripture references: Luke 10:31–37; Acts 6:1–7; 11:28–29; Romans 15:25.

13

The Great Recession and Peter Pan in Retrospect

EVERYTHING SEEMED fine. The giraffes, elephants, tigers, and chimp were leisurely roaming the ranch while the parrot and exotic birds held an idyllic view from the trees. The carnival rides were full of happy children, and the purveyor of the property, the king of the ranch, looked at his investment with pride.

The owner was invigorated in the daytime. However, his inability to cope with past mistakes and a debt overhang of $500 million—combined with lavish spending—made for sleepless nights. He reverted to the use of a type of "pixie dust" called Diprivan because of its anesthetic properties.

His problems remained even though his awareness of them was dulled. To make things worse, those friends who knew the truth remained quiet and enjoyed the illusion of peace while it lasted. With multiple injections of "pixie dust" and a variety of other drugs, it appeared that relief was close at hand and that improved performance, albeit in another country, was only days away. However, after an especially stressful workout for an upcoming gig, reality cast its dark shadow over the empire and its image.

Peter Pan never grew up or responded to an ever-changing environment. He lived in self-denial, believing that all was well in the "land that never was." Analogously, all might seem well in an economy with stocks rising, housing showing some signs of improvement, clunkers being redeemed, job losses lessening, and GDP declining at a slower pace.

From the bailout or outright purchase of banks, insurance companies, and auto firms to quantitative easing and zero interest rates, from the Federal Reserve's rescue efforts to making new homes more affordable, over $7 trillion has been committed to or invested in the economy. All appears to be well as "green shoots" in various forms are spotted by the experts.

The United States will return to economic reality. We will come out of this self-induced euphoria, and, unlike the King of Pop whose financial affairs have fallen into the hands of friend and foe, our country will need to pay for the "pixie dust" it has borrowed from the Chinese, Japanese, British, and others.

The financial injections may bring temporary relief in the equity and housing markets, but unless we face the cause of our inherent weakness—avarice and arrogance—we will return from whence we came. When the anesthesia wears off, we will find ourselves back where we started, or possibly back even further due to the high cost of the drugs.

I am afraid that Peter Pan cannot save us, because he cannot save himself. Trying to live in a self-induced, artificial time warp won't work, and neither will outdated monetary and fiscal policies. *Neverland* was an inflated, exaggerated, ostentatious way of life that had a death sentence on it from the beginning. An economy, or for that matter an individual, must face reality and not avoid it. Moreover, if that means leaving *Neverland* and returning to a "new normal," then so be it. The alternative is to remain starved for more stimulus injections only to be more dependent on drugs with no cure on the horizon.

FOOD FOR THOUGHT

- Is it necessary to be on a particular drug, such as Propofol, to be living under an illusion?

- Why does it seemingly take countries longer than individuals to suffer the ramifications of bad economic or social policies?

- Do we have an obligation to those around us when we see them living lives clouded by deception?

THOUGHT FOR FOOD

- For the amount that the United States is in debt to the rest of the world, see http://www.treasury.gov/ resource-center/data-chart-center/tic/Documents/ mfh.txt.

- Rajan, Raghuram G. *Fault Lines: How Hidden Fractures Still Threaten the World Economy.* Princeton: Princeton University Press, 2011.

- Reinhart, Carmen, and Kenneth Rogoff. *This*

Time Is Different. Princeton: Princeton University Press, 2009. An authoritative book on the "Great Recession."

- Scripture references: Isaiah 64:7; Psalm 79:6; Zephaniah 1:4–6; Romans 8:26; Ephesians 6:17–18; Colossians 1:9–10.

14

Retrospective on the World Trade Center Attack: The Two Wars

Because of the September 11, 2001, attacks on the World Trade Center and the Pentagon, two wars began: the war against terrorism and the war against recession. Both barbarians appeared not only at the gate prior to that tragic date; they were in fact within the walls of our nation, plotting, penetrating, and positioning. Now as a country we have been and are actively fighting these wars, and on separate fronts.

Most of us are aware of the national security measures and directives put in place to fight the war on terrorism. Fewer of us know of the policies enacted to fight the economic downturn that we have encountered during the past several years. Recessions (traditionally defined as two consecutive quarters of negative economic growth, but authoritatively spelled out much more broadly by the Business Cycle Dating Committee of the National Bureau of Economic Research [NBER] at http://www.nber.org/cycles/

recessions.html) can reduce our standard of living, increase our level of personal and national anxiety, decrease our nation's productivity, cause social dysfunction, and make us less competitive internationally.

Even though we no longer currently meet the strictest definition of recession, the economy has been at a virtual standstill and more than likely will exhibit low growth for years to come. The Federal Reserve has affirmed its belief in this extended period of slow or no growth by keeping interest rates at historically low levels through much of 2014. In addition to lower incomes, the upheaval in the stock markets has decreased the net worth of millions of Americans as well as the nation's firms. From 2005 to 2009 inflation-adjusted median wealth fell by 66 percent among Hispanic households and 53 percent among black households, compared to just 16 percent among white households.

Neither the Bush nor the Obama administration intended to allow this slowdown to take a foothold, and both in fact made preemptive strikes, using various fiscal (government spending) and monetary (lower interest rate) weapons to eliminate the possibility of a full-blown downturn. (For a brief look at the monetary instruments of the Federal Reserve, see http://www.federalreserve.gov/monetarypolicy/default.htm. For a comprehensive view of economics, see *Principles of Microeconomics* by N. Gregory Mankiw.)

In the fight against recession, the Federal Reserve and the U.S. government apply widely accepted economic theory. There are no guarantees that government spending, changing tax rates, or Federal Reserve actions will result in success. Japan has implemented many of the same policies to no avail, leaving that nation with a stagnant economy and unemployment that has remained at elevated levels for the past fifteen years. While many economists subscribe to theories supporting tax reductions to encourage investment or federal stimulus policies to promote growth, they do not necessarily believe that absolute truth—truth that can be applied over time with predictable and assured outcomes—exists.

Robert Rubin, former secretary of the U.S. Treasury as well as a former senior executive at both Goldman Sachs and Citigroup, said this very thing in his commencement address at Harvard University in June 2007. Economic principles change with the times and should be adopted merely on a cost-benefit analysis basis. To quote from his address,

> There are no provable certainties. That is the view of modern science and much of modern philosophy. And this view—that there are no absolute or certain answers—quickly leads to recognizing that all significant issues are inherently complex and uncertain and, as a consequence, that all decisions are about probabilities and tradeoffs.

His is an earthly-minded view of reality that bases decisions on tradeoffs with no absolute metric to determine the true costs of those benefits and costs. Everything becomes relative to everything else, and pecuniary values are assigned to non-marketplace items.

I hope, pray, and expect that we will continue to win the war on terrorism as well as the war on this prolonged economic slump. There is, however, no guarantee of a return to the rapid economic growth of the 1990s or its high standard of living. Even so, are there absolute truths from God's Word we can learn regardless of our personal economic situation or that of the country?

If or when we achieve economic victory, will we give God the glory for seeing us through, or will we give full credit to the government and the monetary authorities? I think it is quite clear that blessings, both spiritual and economic, ultimately come from him: "Every good and perfect gift is from above, coming down from the Father of the heavenly lights, who does not change like shifting shadows" (James 1:7).

Another valuable lesson we can learn during difficult times is that of charity. Many people opened their hearts through their bank accounts during the 9/11 season of national sorrow as they also did following hurricane Katrina and the massive 2010 earthquake in Haiti. But does our generosity continue months after the catastrophes? Do our newly sensitized hearts stay that way and continue to respond to human need, both spiritual and material, or does our compassion dissipate, and often quite quickly? Recent evidence shows that donations to the nation's biggest charities dropped 11 percent in 2009, even after the Great Recession ended, marking a decline that was the worst in two decades. We need to be reminded to continue being generous: "Each man should give what he has decided in his heart to give, not reluctantly or under compulsion, for God loves a cheerful giver" (2 Cor. 9:7).

We had, at least for a moment, become a nation that prays. Just as charitable giving decreased, did prayer also take a downturn? I lived in the New York area for nineteen years, and after 9/11 I saw people praying there for the first time. Just like charity, however, commitment to prayer easily dissipates. As soon as it looked as though good economic times were once again around the corner or as though serious threats of terrorism had subsided, our enthusiasm seemed to fizzle. The cycle just seems to start over again: conceit to crisis to Christ to commitment to complacency to conceit—typically we return to where we began, once again depending on ourselves, not God, for the answers to our temporal and eternal dilemmas. His truth and peace are eternal whereas our economic solutions are good only in limited contexts, and then only valid for a season. So, in a limited sense, Robert Rubin did have it right. "Be joyful in hope, patient in affliction, faithful in prayer" (Rom. 12:12).

Finally, even if it were possible to gain the world through economic means, we would lose that which lies within us—that which alone is eternal, our soul (Matt. 16:26).

FOOD FOR THOUGHT

- What causes us to be so prone to forget those in need after their cause no longer warrants front page news?

- Why do lower income households give a greater percent of their income than high-income households?

- How do you respond to someone who believes there are no absolutes? Is it necessary to believe in absolutes to live a "good life"?

- Can you think of some biblical examples of people or groups of people who failed to remember either God's goodness to them or God's people?

THOUGHT FOR FOOD

- Billheimer, Paul E. *Destined for the Throne: How Spiritual Warfare Prepares the Bride of Christ for Her Eternal Destiny.* Minneapolis: Bethany House, 2005. The classic book on prayer and spiritual warfare.

- Foster, Richard J. *Celebration of Discipline: The Path to Spiritual Growth.* New York: HarperCollins, 1998.

- Mankiw, N. Gregory. *Principles of Microeconomics.* 6th ed. Mason, OH: South-Western Cengage Learning, 2011.

- Taylor, Paul, Richard Fry, and Rakesh Kochhar. *Wealth Gaps Rise to Record Highs between Whites, Blacks, Hispanics.* Pew Research Center, July 26, 2011, http://pewsocialtrends.org/2011/07/26/ wealth-gaps-rise-to-record-highs-between-whites-blacks-hispanics. A detailed look at income and wealth disparity.

- Yancey, Philip. *Prayer: Does It Make Any Difference?* Grand Rapids: Zondervan, 2006.

- Zacharias, Ravi. *Why Jesus? Rediscovering His Truth in an Age of Mass Market Spirituality.* Nashville: FaithWords, 2012. One of the world's foremost Christian apologists explains how relativism cannot answer the spiritual hunger in our hearts.

- On how to determine what constitutes a recession, see information on the Business Cycle Dating Committee of the NBER at http://www.nber.org/cycles/recessions.html.

- Scripture references: Acts 4:34–37; 9:36; 10:1–2; 11:29; Romans 15:25–28; 2 Corinthians 8:1–4; 9:6–7.

15

The Heavenly-Minded Economist

MOST ECONOMISTS, or for that matter most academics, errantly think they are doing their analyses in a theological and amoral vacuum. That is, most professors don't consider how much they are being affected by colleagues, mentors, their reading, or scholarly articles—or the degree to which they affect or infect those around them. However, each one—either explicitly or implicitly—is enrolled in a teleological school of thought that sits on a continuum somewhere between love of self and love of God. Each one of us acts according to a thought life that, even at times unconsciously, makes determinations that reflect our hearts. The same could be said for journalists who think their reporting is objective. While that might in fact be the case for a particular article, the decisions regarding what to report on, how to report it, the headline itself, the size of the font used, and the story's placement, whether print or online, all reflect the values of those responsible. It takes both humility and contrition to recognize that we are not the source of truth, nor are we the perfect conveyors of it. These traits are not always found in the well educated.

As Christian economists we must integrate our faith with our economics, but we also must have the conviction that *telos* (i.e., our purpose, goals, and ends) is everything— our chief end in life, that which provides the foundation for our motives and directly affects our means, the methodology by which we approach the economics discipline. Thus, a correctly ordered Christian life will produce results and embrace economics in a way that glorifies God.

An economist whose heart is set on pleasing the Lord and whose mind is under spiritual reconstruction will be enlightened regarding certain unjust economic means of distribution, such as the marketplace of adoption and the market for bodily organs. Cost/benefit analyses and even present value become irrelevant in light of a teleological ordering with God as the ultimate end.

Christian economists need to consider adding a theology grounded in biblical truth concerning Christ and the Trinity to their abilities in sophisticated economic analysis, all within an ecclesiology centered on pleasing God the Father. If they cannot gain that knowledge, they must consider working in tandem with those who have it already. The potential benefit to the economist will be a new or revised orientation away from the secular and temporal economic emphases on consumerism, profit maximization, market solutions, and scarcity toward a *telos* that glorifies the Lord and works itself out in love through acts of goodness and policies that promote goodness in remembrance of God's gift to us through Christ Jesus.

The more we learn to think like him within the boundaries of what is true, noble, right, pure, lovely, admirable, excellent, and praiseworthy while simultaneously avoiding the vain philosophies from the world around us, the better conduits we become for his kingdom principles to be made manifest where we live and his divine will to be accomplished on earth (Matt. 6:10; Phil. 4:8; Col. 3:2). And as we gain the mind of Christ, what earlier had seemed to be an amoral vacuum with little definition now becomes separated into darkness and light.

FOOD FOR THOUGHT

- What is your end goal in life?

- If we have the "mind of Christ," will we consequently agree on major ethical issues?

- Is it possible that economists who aren't following Christ could still hold to ethical and moral convictions in concert with economists who are following the Lord? If so, what coordinates are they using to determine their positions?

THOUGHT FOR FOOD

- For an enlightening and somewhat ecumenical look at economics, see D. Stephen Long, Nancy Ruth Fox, and Tripp York, *Calculated Futures: Theology, Ethics, and Economics* (Waco: Baylor University Press, 2007).

- Scripture references: Philippians 2:5; 4:8; 1 Corinthians 2:16.

16

The Bachelor

TWENTY-FOUR LOSERS and only one winner—that's how it works in the popular television show *The Bachelor*, now in its sixteenth season. And that is the way most people see their own plight. If someone else wins, that means I'm the loser. There is only one prom queen and one prom king, only one valedictorian, only one captain of the squad, only one president of the company, only one senior pastor, and only one gold medalist in a particular sport. In economics this is referred to as a "zero-sum" game. That is, your gain is my loss, and the sum of the two is zero, with no net gain. The implication in the form of a question is this: Why would I want someone else to advance, through promotion, for instance, while their gain simultaneously requires either my demotion or, at best, no advancement for me? Or why would I want to subsidize someone else's education if it means less for me? I suggest that this view should by and large be dismissed.

I wrote this chapter in Shanghai, where along with nine undergraduate students I saw firsthand the negative effects of trade between the United States and China. Thousands of Chinese are working in plants manufacturing goods for U.S. companies to be exported to the United States. This exporting of jobs to China, India, Vietnam, and elsewhere aggravates many Americans, giving them personal justification for their opposition to the expansion of global trade. This opposition, to some degree, is shared by President Obama, as was made evident in his first national address, in which he emphatically and consistently communicated the theme of "buying American." He raised the issue again in his State of the Union address in January 2012 when he said, "We have a huge opportunity, at this moment, to bring manufacturing back. But we have to seize it. Tonight, my message to business leaders is simple: Ask yourselves what you can do to bring jobs back to your country, and your country will do everything we can to help you succeed." I anticipate that the ongoing and severe worldwide economic downturn will cause both industrialized and developing nations, echoing Obama's position, to rethink their trade policies, pushing them toward more mercantilist and nationalistic practices.

Former President Bill Clinton had it partly right when he said in an interview with *Wired* magazine in December 2000 that "the more complex societies get, and the more complex the networks of interdependence within and beyond community and national borders get, the more people are forced in their own interests to find non-zero-sum solutions. That is, win-win solutions instead of win-lose solutions" (available at http://www.wired.com/wired/archive/8.12/clinton.html). This corresponds to modern trade theory, which in essence says that even though a nation is less efficient than all other countries in the production of goods and services, mutually beneficial trade can still take place between that nation and others. Thus trade with China, India, Korea, and Japan need not be feared, because at least theoretically, and in the long run, both parties to the trade will benefit.

Why are we so unwilling to give others credit, applaud those who succeed around us, work enthusiastically and sincerely for the advancement of others, give up personal territory or projects for the common good, or engage in fair trade with other nations? It is because our sinful human nature gravitates toward zero-sum game thinking and action. Psychologists use the term "social trip" to describe a situation in which a group of people acts to obtain short-term personal gains that in the long run lead to a loss for the group as a whole. Why should I even acknowledge your accomplishments or good ideas when doing so might mean less of the pie for me? Why would I even consider "turning the other cheek" or giving to the poor, not requiring a payback for my noteworthy deeds, or sacrificing my life for those who don't even know me, if in the short term personal gain is not evident? All of these positions appear to be losing propositions.

John the Baptist had it right when he said of Jesus, "He must increase, but I must decrease" (John 3:30). John's purpose of "preparing the way" for another greater than himself, along with his eventual martyrdom, did not reduce his significance; it actually increased his importance and transformed his earthly role into an eternal legacy. Without John the Baptist and his acts of selflessness, the kingdom could not have come. Subsequently, the early believers, because of their undivided devotion to Christ, were of the renewed mindset that "holding things in common" was more important than sole proprietorship.

I believe that we need to resist any tendency toward isolationism, both individually and as a nation. This movement toward autarchy could mean cutting off trade ties or refusing to be in fellowship with other Christians. Remember Paul's words, "Now to each one the manifestation of the Spirit is given for the common good" (1 Cor. 12:7). Denying yourself, carrying your cross, applauding others' accomplishments, and being happy for the winner of this season's *Bachelor* (if you were a contestant)—all appear not to be in your self-interest. However, when my interests become what Jesus is interested in, my life takes on more eternal meaning here and now. And in the background he is preparing a place for me and preparing me for that place founded on those acts of love, mercy, and justice in which I have engaged because I love him.

FOOD FOR THOUGHT

- Why is it so difficult to give others credit or see others win?

- If you, your neighbor, or a relative lost a job because of outsourcing, how have you reacted, or how would you react? Will you interpret the job loss in terms of modern trade theory or otherwise?

THOUGHT FOR FOOD

- For a readable book on globalization, see Thomas L. Friedman, *The World Is Flat* (New York: Picador, 2007).

- For a comprehensive book on international trade and finance along with a clear exposition on trade theory, see Dominick Salvatore, *International Economics*, 10th ed. (Hoboken, NJ: Wiley, 2009).

- Scripture references: Acts 2:42; 1 Corinthians 12:12–13.

17

Poverty: What Is It?

Y OU MIGHT think of the United States as the world's
wealthiest country and Haiti as one of the poorest. In
reality, however, prior to the January 12, 2010, earthquake,
Haiti actually ranked 145 out of 169 countries in the Human
Development Index (HDI), the most popular broader mea-
sure of economic well-being. The United States is fourth.
When it comes to income alone, the United States is ninth,
Norway third, and Lichtenstein first. Zimbabwe is last.

So what is poverty? The World Bank's definition of
the poor is those living on less than $1.25 per day. Using
that measure, the world includes 1.4 billion poor people,
down from 1.9 billion in 1981. However, while income is
the most popular measure, it should not be the only metric.
Measures other than the HDI include the Genuine Progress
Indicator (GPI), which adjusts for such factors as income
distribution, the value of household and volunteer work,
the costs of crime, and pollution. An even more heterodox
approach is the "happiness index," the scores for which are
based on responses to questions about satisfaction with

life. Using this measure, Costa Rica is the globe's "happiest" country, while Togo, a country in West Africa, is the least.

The Bible includes numerous examples of spiritual, absolute, and relative poverty. The "prodigal," or lost, son was spiritually, physically, and emotionally famished. The story of Joseph's brothers, who came in search of grain and food to keep their families from starvation during the years of famine, provides us with an example of absolute poverty. An example of relative poverty may be seen in James's admonishment to the church regarding its discriminatory practice of giving particular socio-economic groups preferred seating in church services.

The most important type of poverty, and one I believe we must recognize within ourselves in order to be truly wealthy, is spiritual poverty. Claiming that we are rich, self-made people who need nothing and no one, able to pull ourselves up by our own bootstraps, marks us as spiritually destitute (Rev. 3:17). So while it seems a paradox that one can be rich and poor at the same time, this line of thinking is in fact orthodox; if we don't admit how poor we are without Christ, he is unable to show us the incomparable riches of grace we receive when we are in him (Eph. 1:7). On the other hand, no matter how economically poor you might be or become in this world, as his child you will forever experience God's love in abundance through his only Son, Jesus.

FOOD FOR THOUGHT

- Are you satisfied with your life? What measures do you use to determine whether you are or not?

- Do you consider income and wealth as the most

important measures of well being? Why do most Americans think of income as the main determinant of satisfied life?

- Why are we slow to understand or admit "spiritual poverty"?

THOUGHT FOR FOOD

- See the "World Database of Happiness," http://worlddatabaseofhappiness.eur.nl/index.html.

- See the "Human Development Index," http://hdr.undp.org/en.

- Scripture references: Psalm 140:12; Isaiah 25:4; Luke 4:18–19; 1 John 3:17–19.

18

Life's Most Important Lesson

PERHAPS THE most important application of economics to the Scriptures is the idea of opportunity cost, defined as the cost of the sacrificed alternative. That is, what have I sacrificed in order to gain something else? I like to think of this as "opportunity lost." An example: if I sleep in tomorrow morning and don't go to work, I certainly will gain some extra sleep; however, I might lose my job in the process. Or if I go to work at the office over the weekend instead of going to my son's or daughter's sporting event, I will lose out on a shared family experience.

Matthew 16:26 records Jesus's question, "What will it profit a man if he gains the whole world and loses his soul? Or what will a man give in exchange for his soul?" This is a picture of an all-or-nothing situation. Grasping the meaning of Jesus's words also requires that we define "profit" (i.e., either in terms of material gain or spiritual gain). Jesus more than implies that true profitability is not referring to the so-called "bottom line" or to net accounting profit, nor is he referring to social responsibility

72

or environmental sustainability or "green" measures like LEED Certification. Jesus is instead referring to the spiritual bottom line, which cuts to the heart—and indeed the soul—of my existence now and forever. Do I want to give up my eternal home for a temporary and rapidly depreciating mansion? In this situation I have gained the world and all the pleasures that entails. But what have I lost in the process? I have forfeited my eternal soul and exchanged it for that which is temporal—including my house, boat, television, iPod, books, career, club membership, bank account, and on and on. The wise person will determine the opportunity cost in advance and ask the question, "What am I giving up in order to gain this temporal pleasure or pursuit?" If we could see the big picture and recognize the eternal benefits that we would be relinquishing, we would never (rationally) accept the tradeoff.

FOOD FOR THOUGHT

- Maybe you have never considered life's biggest question: What about my soul? Eternal life with Christ is possible only if I understand that I am a sinner; that Jesus provides the only way of salvation through his death and resurrection; and that by repenting of my sins and believing and professing that the work of Christ—his sinless life and loving death for me—provides the forgiveness for those sins, I will be saved from eternal separation from him and live with him in his kingdom for eternity.

- If you are a Christian, consider those things in

your life you have refused or neglected to count the opportunity cost; i.e., have you traded God's blessing, peace, and joy in your life for some temporal, short-lived enjoyment? On the other hand, have you contemplated something that might have brought personal gratification but that, when considered in light of what you would be giving up in terms of God's blessing, has lost its lustre?

THOUGHT FOR FOOD

- See "Spiritual Capital" at http://www.researchmethods.org/sci/sci.htm.
- Scripture references: Matthew 10:39; Mark 8:35.

19

The Price of Bean Soup

THERE IS a much-used concept in microeconomics called "elasticity of demand," a measure that is at the same time theoretical and practical and yet essentially mathematical. The principle of elasticity states that given a percentage change in price (either an increase or a decrease), there is an associated percentage change in the quantity demanded of that particular good or service. Let's say that the price of a good goes up ten percent but the demand for that good goes down twenty percent. This case would be regarded as "elastic." That is, the demand for that good is highly sensitive to a change in price. If you were the seller, you might think twice before raising your price because your total revenues would decline. On the other hand, we might raise the price of a good by ten percent and the demand for that good might go down by only five percent. This good would be described in economic terms as being "price inelastic," reflecting an insensitivity to changes in price. The less sensitive to price changes, the more inelastic (or the less elastic) the demand for that commodity will be. That is why, in general, travelers who want to fly at the last minute pay more for airline tickets than leisure travelers who have some flexibility in their schedules. We are also are typically more sensitive to increases in the prices of items that are costly rather than inexpensive. For example, we probably won't cut back our purchase of table salt it the price increases by fifteen percent, but if the price of a $30,000 car were to go up by the same percentage we would take notice, perhaps negatively affecting our desire to purchase the automobile.

Now think about the story of Jacob and Esau from Genesis 25:29–34, an account particularly familiar to those of you who were raised in a church that included children's Sunday school. Jacob is cooking some stew when his brother Esau comes in, famished from the open country. He begs Jacob to give him some of the red stew, to which his crafty brother responds that he will do so in exchange for his "older" twin's birthright. "I'm about to die!" Esau declares. "What good is my birthright to me?" Jacob demands an oath, and the deal is made. Esau eats, drinks, gets up, and leaves. "So Esau," we read, "despised his birthright."

Esau was absolutely insensitive to the price of soup. We might say in economic terms that he exhibited very inelastic demand. The soup on the open market in a typical situation would have cost him only a few dollars, but because of the circumstances (the immediacy of his hunger), he was willing to pay for a bowl of soup (or stew) at any price. As a result he gave away not only the double monetary advantages of the birthright but also the spiritual advantages of being patriarch, priest, and chief of the Abrahamic lineage—all for a short-term but seemingly insatiable need.

Sound familiar? Don't we all get into situations where we act irrationally, illogically, and unspiritually? Don't we, like Esau, enjoy short-term pleasure while relinquishing long-term gain? What are the consequences of trading our blessings, those good things God has for us, both current and future, to fill our stomachs, minds, bank accounts, and so on—just because we "needed it now"? If someone craves drugs, sex, or power, will they be insensitive to the cost of their objective, possibly going so far as to pay *anything*, including murder, loss of family, alienation of friends, or loss of freedom?

What is the solution? Trying to get our eyes off the short-run situation. This is difficult to do since our hunger for things that lie outside God's boundaries for living (and ultimately lead to death) cause us to respond in a less than godly fashion. So are we willing to forsake long-term blessings for short-term satisfaction? "Teach us to number our days, that we may gain a heart of wisdom" (Ps. 90:12).

FOOD FOR THOUGHT

- Think back to a wrong decision you made because you lacked a long-term perspective on the outcome.

- Write down three things you can do to protect yourself from circumstances that might lead to short-sighted decision making.

THOUGHT FOR FOOD

- Barton, Ruth Haley. *Strengthening the Soul of Your Leadership.* Downers Grove, IL: InterVarsity, 2008. While this is primarily a book for those in leadership, the principles apply to all who are seeking Godly direction.

- Huffman, Douglas S. *How Then Should We Choose? Three Views on God's Will and Decision Making.* Grand Rapids: Kregel, 2009.

- Meadors, Gary T. *Decision Making God's Way: A New Model for Knowing God's Will.* Grand Rapids: Baker Books, 2003.

- Scripture references: Psalm 37:34; Matthew 25:22–23; Acts 24:24–27; Romans 2:6–8; 1 Corinthians 10:13; 2 Timothy 4:7–8; James 1:2–4.

20

Fellowship and Free Trade

ARE COUNTRIES better off with free trade, or should they restrict trade? Should a country even go to the extreme of living in isolation? That is, should it live in autarchy, with no relationships with other sovereign nations?

For many years it was believed that a country should encourage exports and limit imports because a nation could become stronger only if it exported more than it imported. The justification for this belief was that a nation's wealth was determined by the amount of gold it held. Therefore, if imports were greater than exports (a negative balance in the current account), this deficit was essentially paid for in gold, reducing the nation's reserve and thereby reducing its wealth. Given the limited amount of gold in the world and the belief that trade was a zero-sum game (my gain is equal to your loss), this perspective promoted nationalism if not outright protectionism. This was the thinking of the mercantilists in the sixteenth and seventeenth centuries.

Adam Smith, the father of economics, held a different view in the late eighteenth century. He and other classical economists were concerned about the basis for trade, the gains from trade, and why nations would restrict trade if in fact there were gains to be realized from it. Smith wondered why losing nations would voluntarily participate in trade. To him the mercantilists were illogical in their thinking because trade was in fact taking place. He believed that trade was based on absolute advantage, that is, if a nation were more efficient (had an absolute advantage) than another nation in the production of a commodity, it paid for that nation to specialize in the production of the commodity and exchange the excess production for the commodity of its absolute disadvantage (the good it was less efficient in producing)—to the benefit of both nations. Smith advocated free trade, allowing for the exceptions of protecting infant industries or of national defense.

Then came along the law of comparative advantage, which was explained initially by David Ricardo (1817) using the labor theory of value, and later (1931) and more acceptably by Haberler using opportunity cost theory. This law states that even if a nation is less efficient than another in the production of both commodities (assuming it to be a two-commodity nation), there is still a basis for mutually advantageous trade as long as the absolute advantage that one nation has over the other is not the same in both commodities. The nation that is less efficient than another in the production of both commodities (i.e., the nation that has an absolute disadvantage in both commodities) should specialize and export the commodity in which its absolute disadvantage is least or less (this is the area of its comparative advantage) and import the commodity in which its absolute disadvantage is greater (the area of its comparative disadvantage). This law holds if the absolute advantage one nation has over another is not the same in both commodities, which would mean that the nation with an absolute disadvantage in both commodities would not have a comparative advantage in either commodity.

If we have specialization and trade, each nation will be better off even if one nation is less efficient in the production of either commodity. Think about the following two-country, two-commodity example. Assume that the United States can produce three cars in one hour or, alternatively, four units of food in one hour, and that Japan can produce two cars or one unit of food in one hour. The United States, therefore, is more efficient in the production of both items. That is, it can produce both more cars and more food than Japan can in an hour's time. Will we still have trade between the countries?

Let's think in terms of opportunity cost, upon which the law of comparative advantage is based. The cost of cars in terms of food given up (opportunity cost) in the United States is 4/3 foods (divide both cars and food by three to put it in terms of one car), and the cost of cars in terms of food given up in Japan is 1/2 foods (divide both cars and food by two to put it in terms of one car).

The brain surgeon could mow her lawn or clean her house, but what is the cost of mowing her own lawn or cleaning her own home? The cost is what she could otherwise be doing, which in this case would be performing life-saving surgery. Thus the cost to the brain surgeon of mowing her own lawn is very high, and she should consider specializing in brain surgery and hiring someone else to mow her lawn. Likewise Japan is giving up less in terms of food to produce cars than the United States and therefore should specialize in this commodity and export it to the United States in exchange for food. In terms of the food the United States is giving up, it costs 3/4 of a car to produce one unit of food. Japan, at the same time, is giving up two cars to produce one unit of food. The United States is giving up less in terms of cars than the Japanese and therefore should specialize and trade in this commodity.

It makes sense, then, for the United States to trade food for cars with Japan. If the terms of trade are four units of food for four cars, the limits of trade, in terms of food, are three cars < four units of food < eight cars. That is, the United States will want to trade for more than three cars to be better off, and Japan will not trade for more than eight cars to prevent ending up worse off. So trade will take place somewhere between three and eight cars. Then the United States can specialize in the production of its comparative advantage, which is food, producing four units (assuming constant costs, neither increasing nor decreasing with the next unit produced) and trading these four units of food for four Japanese cars.

The four cars would have taken the United States one hour to produce, meaning that the United States gains one car because domestically it can produce only three cars in one hour. Japan would specialize in cars, manufacture four, and trade the cars for four units of food. Is Japan better off? It would have taken Japan four hours to produce the four units of food. If they would have used these four hours to manufacture cars, they could have produced eight cars. Thus they have a net gain of four cars. The gain for the entire world (we are restricting ourselves to two countries for simplicity of explanation) is five cars. Trade benefits everyone, even those who have no comparative advantage in the production of any commodity.

Now let's think in terms of a person deciding to live their spiritual life in isolation. It has been said many times that we don't need to be in church or to fellowship with other believers because we can sufficiently worship God while fishing at the banks of the river or on a golf course. No one would argue that the Lord is not present at the river's edge or on the eighth hole; however, aren't we better off worshiping with other followers of Jesus rather than in isolation?

From an economic standpoint, when you attend church you are trading your spiritual gifts with others who are also in attendance. On your own you can sing songs to the Lord, read and meditate upon the Scriptures, and pray effective prayers, all of which are very beneficial. However, if you take these gifts to a place where other believers are gathered and share them either in a small or large group setting, others also benefit from the gifts God has given you.

Paul reminds us that spiritual gifts are not to be used in isolation but for mutual benefit: "Now to each one the manifestation of the Spirit is given for the common good" (1 Cor. 12:7). Paul also refers to "weaker" gifts and points out that some individuals who had these seemingly less desirable gifts, abilities, or talents believed that they were not needed by the larger body or were looked down upon by those with more demonstrative gifts. To the contrary, we know from the law of comparative advantage that even if we possess the same gifts as others we still have a reason to fellowship (trade) with them. If we each specialize in the area of our comparative advantages (those gifts and ministries at which we are relatively better in terms of opportunity cost than some others) and use those gifts for the common good, while receiving from others those gifts and ministries in which we have comparative disadvantages (those areas with the greatest opportunity cost for us), the body of Christ will be built up.

A goal for each believer is to discern their optimal gifts and ministries (come to the realization that they are a hand, foot, eye, etc.) and recognize that they may have multiple gifts and talents in varying degrees. This requires that they calculate the opportunity cost of each gift in terms of the others. Those gifted in numerous areas must relegate their time to the areas in which they are the most productive. For those who have only one "small" gift, the tendency might be to not exercise it, to keep it hidden, and to feel less important than those with the "greater" gifts. But Paul's admonition is both strong and direct: if God himself gives more honor to the "parts that lack it," we should do the same (giving greater honor to the weaker and treating the "less presentable parts" with great modesty).

Finally, we should acknowledge that fellowship is a necessity in the Christian life and that by living in isolation, we reduce the ability of the body of Christ to grow (in economic terms, overall or "world" production would decline). We need to recognize as well that both we and our fellow believers will fail to benefit from our God-given ministries (individual consumption will decrease due to lack of specialization and trade). Even if we were to posit that there are no duplications of gifts and ministries in the body of Christ, the tenet still holds that living in autarchy would reduce both the variety of gifts available (production) and the ministry of those gifts to others (consumption). All in all, we would end up with a "poorer," less productive church.

FOOD FOR THOUGHT

- Why do many people desire to live in isolation, especially when it comes to their unwillingness to attend church on a regular basis?

- How do we view those individuals who are multitalented or multi-gifted? How do they view themselves?

- How do people with few talents view themselves? What can those around them do to encourage their participation in the church and elsewhere?

THOUGHT FOR FOOD

- Coase, R. H. *Essays on Economics and Economists.* Chicago: University of Chicago Press, 1994. A readable perspective on Adam Smith's work and that of other notable economists from the perspective of a Nobel Prize winner.

- Smith, Adam. *An Inquiry into the Nature and Causes of the Wealth of Nations.* 1776; New York: Oxford University Press, 2008.

- Warren, Rick. *The Purpose Driven Church: Every Church Is Big in God's Eyes.* Grand Rapids: Zondervan, 1995. A discussion of the purpose and benefits of the Christian church.

21

Supply-Side Christianity

CAN A parent ask too much of a child, a teacher of a student, or an employer of an employee, to the point that the individual is discouraged, de-motivated, shies away from work or responsibility, and/or loses interest in the topic or task at hand? Can church leaders demand too much from their congregations and youth groups, so as to exasperate them?

One of the four basic tenets of supply-side economics is that if we reduce the marginal tax rates on individuals, they will increase their willingness and ability to work, causing them to earn more, save more, and invest more. That is, if my next dollar earned is to be taxed at 20 percent instead of 30 percent, I will be more willing to work longer hours and also increase my productivity. I will be keeping more of the income I have produced, and overall the government's tax revenues will increase due to the fact that my increase in taxable income is greater than the reduction in the marginal tax rate, thereby increasing government revenues. Bottom line: everyone is better off. Another principle of supply-side economics is that of deregulation. Too much regulation stifles competition, reduces productivity, and ultimately has a negative effect upon the consumer. By deregulating we free up industries to better respond to the needs of their customers. Examples of deregulation in the United States include rail and truck transportation, airlines, telecommunications, finance, and energy.

What does the Bible say about heavy burdens and the requirements of Christianity upon its followers? As recorded in Matthew 11:30, Jesus says this: "For my yoke is easy and my burden is light." I understand this to mean that following Jesus is neither impossible nor impractical, nor is it hampered by obstacles that prohibit us from accomplishing what he wants for and from us.

The Council at Jerusalem, composed of the early church's apostles and elders, sent this message (recorded by Luke in Acts 15:28–29) to the gentile believers living in Antioch, Syria, and Cilicia: "It seemed good to the Holy Spirit and to us not to burden you with anything beyond the following requirements: You are to abstain from food sacrificed to idols, from blood, from the meat of strangled animals and from sexual immorality. You will do well to avoid these things. Farewell."

It seems that the regulations upon new believers (at least the gentiles) in the New Testament were reduced to four basic issues. We could easily argue about what is meant by the above guidelines, but I believe we can infer that the leaders of the New Testament church were determined not to place too heavy a burden on the converts nor to return to Jewish law. And isn't the burden of overregulation exactly what's wrong with legalism—form without function, rules without revival, laws without life? In contrast, following Christ is liberating not only in the sense that we are no longer "slaves to sin" or bound by tradition nor Old Testament law but in that we are now free to serve him.

An example of an excessive burden can be seen in the plight of many third-world countries burdened with a so-called "debt overhang." The theory is that if a country has too much debt and little possibility of reducing that debt internally through economic growth, there is little likelihood it can either pay back its debt to other nations or creditors or grow internally. Thus, the IMF and World Bank at times grant "debt forgiveness," or relief, to those nations that otherwise could not service the debt and also make the necessary investments in their own economies. This is similar to U.S. bankruptcy laws, in which the individual or corporation is given various degrees of protection or relief from creditors so that they can get a "fresh start," without which they would have little or no chance of economic survival.

The lesson for us: we have received forgiveness of sins, freeing us to do the right thing by refusing to return to a life of rules and regulations in which we attempt to run a race against other people who are also trying to establish their own righteousness. Second, we are not to place undue burdens and regulations on those around us, making them strive toward goals and objectives that we ourselves have not met and will never meet.

FOOD FOR THOUGHT

- Can you identify examples in your life of excessive requirements or unrealistic expectations that were frustrating, if not counterproductive, for you?

- Can you think back to times when your own overregulation might have frustrated the progress of family members or those working with or for you?

- In Ephesians 6:4 Paul admonishes, "Parents, do not exasperate your children; instead, bring them up in the training and instruction of the Lord." To what type of training and instruction is he referring? It's the kind that produces both a willingness to serve and obey and a joy in doing so, motivated by our desire to please the Creator who loves us. If we as parents love our children "in the Lord," they will obey us, knowing that we are looking out for their souls.

THOUGHT FOR FOOD

- For a closer look at supply-side economics, see Bruce R. Bartlett, *Reagonomics* (New York: Arlington House, 1981).

- For a video on supply-side economics by Arthur Laffer, see http://www.youtube.com/watch?v=BrfyR5V46zs.

- See Nobel winner Robert Mundell's take on supply-side economics at http://robertmundell.net/nobel-prize.

- For information on IMF debt relief and policies, see http://www.imf.org/external/np/exr/facts/hipc.htm.

- For information on bankruptcy laws, see http://
  www.uscourts.gov/FederalCourts/Bankruptcy.aspx.

22

You're Hired!

SITTING AT a table of college students who would be graduating that spring semester, I asked them what type of job prospects they had. Not one had anything solid. I went on to suggest that the first step in their job search might be to pray. I recognize that this might have sounded simplistic and presumptive, something your grandmother or grandfather would tell you, but I believe that we please our Lord by going to him first. Considering that he is our loving Heavenly Father, doesn't it follow that we should lay before him our most important life decisions?

Over two-hundred years ago Robert Thomas Malthus predicted that population growth would outstrip the food supply, resulting in misery and poverty. This "Malthusian Trap" did not occur due to significant increases in agricultural productivity and slowed population growth, especially in higher-income countries. Malthus will always be remembered, however, along with Thomas Carlyle, for helping give economics the derogatory label "the dismal science" on the basis of this bleak outlook.

Are college graduates subject to a similar type of Malthusian Trap, whereby it appears that due to the economic downturn, there is little hope of finding employment? Are their future jobs and careers inextricably linked to the natural world? Or do they serve and follow the One who can "provide a table in the wilderness"? Is Jesus able to provide meaningful work for our students in the midst of a global recession, or is he constrained by the same economic principles and laws of nature that we face? If he can heal the sick, raise the dead, walk on water, and, most important, forgive our sins, isn't Jesus also able to guide us in our career paths?

I believe that God will provide for us in all of the desert places in our lives, and that includes those anxious periods of a job search or those lonely intervals of unemployment. There is sufficient evidence of God's provision, both in the Scriptures and in the lives of those who have believed in him throughout the ages. Sometimes it's a matter of taking what little remaining faith you might have—both in yourself and in his ability to answer your prayers—offering that faith up to him, and allowing him to work. When he does provide a job, your first order of business will be to thank him, acknowledging that "every good and perfect gift is from above."

FOOD FOR THOUGHT

- When you pray for a job or career, do you believe that the Lord is actually interested enough to guide and provide?

- Are you willing not only to pray for those who

need a job but also inform them that you are praying for their situation and believe that God will answer your prayer?

- What is your local church doing to help the unemployed or underemployed? What suggestions do you have that might benefit those fellow believers?

THOUGHT FOR FOOD

- For more information on employment and unemployment statistics, see http://www.bls.gov.

- For books on career paths, see *LinchPin* (New York: Portfolio, 2010) and *Tribes* (New York: Portfolio, 2008), both by Seth Godin.

23

Driven by Faith or Fear?

THE WORLD seems to be increasingly driven by fear; governments in particular are making economic decisions based on their fear of what might be around the corner. The Dow Jones Industrial Average is making daily knee-jerk reactions to media headlines, especially those that increase uncertainty about the future. This is why measures of consumer confidence are so closely watched; to a large degree they reflect the amount of fear or faith individuals have in their economic future. So if you and I are afraid of losing our jobs or of being unable to find employment, we will cut back on our spending. This is especially important to economies such as the United States because our consumer spending is approximately 70 percent of the overall economy—so goes our personal spending, so goes the economy. Fear results in inaction or retraction, leading to a reduction of spending and investment that negatively affects national income, reduces productivity, and diminishes expectations for future growth.

Economic fear has driven and continues to drive the proposals coming from both Washington and the European Union, and for good reason. Unemployment, if you include in the picture discouraged and underemployed workers, stood at 16.2 percent in 2011. Jobless claims have been up and down; however, the number of those continuing to receive jobless benefits remains elevated. Bankruptcy filings have increased 14 percent nationwide since 2007. In 2010 there were 1.53 million personal bankruptcies, up 9 percent from 2009. In addition, there were 157 bank failures in 2010, up from 139 in 2009. The reality of a double dip in housing prices or recession is always at the door, causing paralysis in spending by individuals and corporations. Six major markets have hit their lowest levels since home prices started to fall in 2006 and 2007, while housing starts are down 64 percent from ten years ago. As a result of lower equity in your home, you are less likely to spend on nonessential items and also unable to take out as much equity from your home as you could have before to finance home renovations or pay for your child's education.

Consumer confidence is down, world merchandise trade is slowing, and the dollar is on its biggest "losing streak" since 2004. Total state budget shortfalls are around $160 billion, and the U.S. debt is over $14 trillion, with foreigners holding $4.5 trillion of that amount.

Fear for the future and the reality of the present are combining to drive governments and central banks worldwide to continue injecting legally-approved financial steroids into their economic systems. And if the stimulus money in the European Union happens to run dry, China has stated that it is prepared to use its $2.7 trillion in reserves to bail out the troubled EU countries; as recently as late 2011 it had talks with Italy about the possibility of bailing out the world's eighth-largest economy. Japan had also previously agreed to rescue the European Union if necessary. The objective of these unprecedented actions by the world's largest economies is to restore confidence so as to encourage consumer spending and business investment.

As it does a nation, fear can inhibit our effectiveness and progress as individuals. It moves us backward in our journey with the Lord, and that is why we need to overcome it. We don't do so by government fiat but by faith in God and his Word.

You can fear the past, the present, or the future. You can fear things seen or unseen. You can fear failure or even success. You can fear living or dying or both. You can fear other people. You can fear either doing God's will or not doing it.

"I will fear no evil, for you are with me," declares the psalmist (Ps. 23:4). Paul told Timothy that "God's Spirit does not make us timid but gives us power" (2 Tim. 1:7). When Jesus's disciples saw him walking on the lake in the storm, Jesus told them not to be afraid. John reminds us that "there is no fear in love because perfect love drives out fear." We can go to sleep at night in peace, without fear, because "the Lord makes us dwell in safety" (Ps. 4:8).

FOOD FOR THOUGHT

- Can you relate to David's prayer in Psalm 23? Do you think he ever overcame fear immediately?

- Are being confident and exuding confidence two different things?

- Why do we fear people and circumstances? Are these fears always unfounded?

- What are some ways to increase our confidence in the Lord so that we can more effectively accomplish those tasks that he is asking us to do?

THOUGHT FOR FOOD

- For more on consumer confidence measures, see http://www.conference-board.org/data/consumerdata.cfm; http://thomsonreuters.com/products_services/financial/financial_products/a-z/umichigan_surveys_of_consumers; or http://research.stlouisfed.org/fred2/series/UMCSENT.

- For more information on GDP and consumer spending, see http://www.bea.gov/national/index.htm.

- For information regarding foreign holders of U.S. debt, see http://www.treasury.gov/resource-center/data-chart-center/tic/Documents/mfh.txt.

- Scripture references: Proverbs 29:25; Luke 12:4–5; Philippians 1:27–28; 2 Timothy 1:6–7.

24

The Bronze Medal

OVER THE past twenty years I have consulted many individuals who are interested in careers in the music industry. The list includes musicians, vocalists, and those who want to work on the business side of the industry. In several cases they have appeared to be quite unrealistic about the level of notoriety they will attain or their expected sphere of influence. Many want to be the next U2, Coldplay, or Carrie Underwood. Others desire to work for such famous venues as Radio City Music Hall, and still others aspire to playing drums for the likes of Keith Urban or Switchfoot. It's possible that some will become American or worldwide idols, but others, the vast majority, will end up in seemingly more mundane positions in life, experiencing a level of success not matching their aspirations or expectations.

The same is true of countries. Small, less-developed countries do not have the same economic influence that large, developed countries exert. For example, there are only a few countries whose currencies are considered "world currencies," in that they can be used as payment for any other country's exports. Also, it's improbable that a

small country can affect exchange rates or have much lever-
age when it comes to trade barriers such as tariffs or voluntary export restraints. Even though its circle of influence
is much smaller than that of a large, industrialized nation,
however, the small country still has importance, purpose,
and an ability to provide a healthy structure for its people to
prosper. However, this country will not be a major influenc-
er in world political or economic affairs. It must live within
its borders while striving to move concentrically outward
in terms of higher standards of living and freedoms for its
people. According to Derek Prince, maturity is to live with
the actual but hold on to the ideal. The same holds true for
countries.

When you "reach for the stars and only catch the
moon," you might be inclined to think less of yourself and
end up being discouraged or disillusioned. I think the apostle Paul can help bring balance to our thinking regarding
our life goals and aspirations when he warns us not to think
too highly of ourselves but to use sound and sober judgment when it comes to our gifts and abilities (Rom. 12).
Otherwise, when we don't meet those unrealistic and sometimes false expectations, or when we become impatient in
our journey, the experience can be de-motivating and even
cause us to retrench in our pursuit of what the Lord has for
us. Somewhere along the way, with good advice from those
around us and by listening to the Holy Spirit, we come to
better understand the tension of pursuing the "promised
land" while still living in tents (Heb. 11). There might also
come a realization that "we still haven't found what we're
looking for" because we're looking in all the wrong places.
Direction and affirmation of God's plan for our lives will

become clear only when we regularly, willingly, and honestly present ourselves to him as living sacrifices.

If this book has helped you understand some of the basic principles of economics more clearly, I will have accomplished one of my goals. And if through these readings you are somehow closer to living a life that is more open and honest before Jesus, then he is more likely to accomplish his goals through you.